HOPE HOUSE OF POWER APOSTOLIC CHURCH, INC.

I0463714

POST OFFICE BOX 331

SAVANNAH, TN 38372

731-412-8961

731-925-4597

BUSNIESS PLAN FOR CHURCH/MINISTRIES OUTREACH

THE RESCUE MISSION MINISTRY- SHALL HOLD SINGLE MEN AND WOMEN AND FAMILIES WITH UP TO (1) CHILD; OUR

SETUP SHALLL BE QUASI APARTMENT AND DORM LIKE SETTINGS; ALL SHALL STAY IN THE DORM OR QUASI APARTMENT IF FAMILY UP TO 1 CHILD; NOT LONGER

THAN 6 MONTHS
FOR EMPLOYMENT
SEEKERS AND NOT
LONGER THAN 12
MONTHS FOR
SSI/SSDI/STATE
BENEFICIARIES. ALL
MEN/WOMEN 18
AND OLDER SHALL

HAVE CHORES AND THEY ARE TO BE DONE AND DONE CORRECTLY. ALL 18 AND OLDER SHALL HAVE NEGATIVE/POSITIVE WRITE UP CHARTS;

THREE STRIKES; YOUR OUT RULE!

ALL ARE SUBJECT TO CHURCH SERVICES/DEVOTION; SUNDAY(MORNING OR EVENING) IS MANDATORY; THREE CHAPEL SERVICES

ATTENDANCE IS (EXCEPT SATURDAY) MANDATORY. ALL RESIDENTS SHALL SEEK EMPLOYMENT OR GO TO THEIR LEGAL REP AND THE SSA OFFICE AND BRING BACK A

LETTER FROM EACH
STATING THEY WERE
AT THAT CERTAIN
PLACE FOR THE DAY.
ALL RESIDENTS ARE
APPOINTED A BED
AREA TO WHICH
THEY SHALL KEEP
CLEAN; ALONG WITH

THEIR BODIES AND CLOTHES. OUR RESCUE MISSION; WE HOPE TO BE A 1-5 FLOOR BUILDING ; WHERE THE 1ST FLOOR SHALL BE THE ADMINISTRATIVE

AREA FOR

OFFICERS;STAFF;

MINISTERS AND

VISITORS ONLY!!

OUR SOUP KITCHEN-

SHALL BE THE AREA

OF MORNING;NOON

AND EVENING

MEALS. ALL MEALS

SHALL BE EATEN

WITHIN THE HOUR.

NO TRESPASSERS

SHALL BE ALLOWED;

NO MOOCHING; NO

PANHANDLING AND

NO LOITERING. ALL

MEALS SHALL BE

EATEN IN THE SOUP

KITCHEN/FOODSTUFF NO FOOD IN BED AREA ALLOWED EVER!; NO FELLOWSHIPPING IN THE DOORWAY. ALL SHALL BE ALLOWED RESTROOM FACILITY USAGE BEFORE AND

AFTER THEIR MEAL IS COMPLETED. MEALS WILL BE SERVED ON A FIRST COME/FIRST SERVE BASIS. 2 MEALS MUST BE HOT MEALS. LUNCH MAY/MAY NOT BE SERVED BROWN

BAG. ALL MUST BE 21
YEARS OF AGE TO
ENTER. NO CHILDREN
ALLOWED
WHATSOEVER
UNDER THE AGE OF
21.
CHURCH- SHALL BE
TO HOLD RELIGIOUS

MEETINGS/SERVICES

FOR BOTH PUBLIC

AND PRIVATE. THE

RESIDENTS SHALL

HAVE ASSIGNED

SEATING. WE SHALL

HOLD CHRISTIAN

STANDARD SERVICES

INCLUDING THE

RITES OF MARRIAGE; WATER BAPTISM IN JESUS NAME; AND FUNERALS FOR THE BEREAVED FAMILIES;ORDAIN NEW MINISTERS AND DEDICATIONS OF INFANTS AND

CHILDREN. NO ONE OF THE ALTERNATIVE LIFESTYLES SHALL /WILL BE ALLOWED TO HOLD OFFICE OR USED IN THE PULPIT FOR WHATSOEVER REASON; NEITHER SHALL THEY BE

EMPLOYED WITHIN OUR FACILITIES. WE WILL MARRY ONLY ONE MAN TO ONE WOMAN. WE SHALL KEEP THE STRICTEST OF FINANCIAL RECORDS INCLUDING/UP TO:

TITHES/OFFERINGS/ LOVE OFFERINGS.

NEWSLETTER OFFICE- THIS SHALL BE OUR OFFICIAL PUBLIC NOTICE TO THE PUBLIC/PRIVATE/ RELIGIOUS INSTITUTION

CENTERS-THIS WILL

INFORM THE PUBLIC

OF ALL ACTIVITIES

WITHIN AND

WITHOUT THE

MINISTRY

INCLUDING

COMMENTS/

PICTURES AND

ANNOUNCEMENTS

OF WHO GOT THEIR

AWARD LETTERS OR

EMPLOYMENT AND

WILL BE MOVING

OUT SOON!!

DELIVERANCE

CENTER- THIS

CENTER SHALL BE

FOCUSED ON THE NARCOTIC/ALCOHOL ABUSERS THROUGH A SIX MONTH PROGRAM WITH DOCTORS AND NURSES AND CLERGY. ALL RESIDENTS SHALL

WORK FOR THE MINISTRY FACILITIES INCLUDING HAVING CHORES; ATTEND DAILY RELIGIOUS MEETINGS; CHAPEL;DEVOTIONS; AND AS NEEDED ATTEND TO PHSYC

AND MEDICAL EVALS.
ALL MEMBERS ONCE
IN THEIR ROOMS
MUST WAIT FOR THE
DOOR TO BE OPENED
BY STAFF. NO
VISITORS WILL BE
ALLOWED FOR THE
ENITRE 6 MONTHS.

ALL RESIDENTS WILL

SIGN A PROMISSORY

NOTE TO PAY A

$4200 UNITED

STATES DOLLAR DEBT

TO THE MINISTRY

FOR THEIR STAY

WITHIN 2 YEARS (48

MONTHS) AS A LOVE

OFFERING.

MEDICAL CLINIC- NO

RESIDENT WHO

CANNOT PAY WILL

BE WITHOUT A

DOCTOR; NURSE; OR

MEDICINE.

RESIDENTS SHALL

PAY ON A SLIDING SCALE FEE; RESIDENTS SHALL SIGN A PROMISSORY NOTE TO PAY IN 2 YEARS THE BILLS THEY INCUR PATICULARLY THOSE ON SOCIAL SECURITY.

HOSPITAL (24/7/365)-EVEN IF PATIENT CANNOT PAY. EVERY TEST WILL BE DONE/ PHYSICALLY POSSIBLE. WE PLAN FOR ALL PHYSICAL/SPIRITUAL

/MENTAL/FINANCIAL /EMOTIONAL/DIET NEEDS AND COUNSEL TO BE INVOKED/MET/GAVE WHEN WANTED/NEEDED. UNIVERSITY- GED CLASSES SHALL BE

GIVEN FOR THOSE NEEDING A GED; A COLLEGE COURSE OR 2 SHALL BE ADMINISTERED TO GET THE BALL ROLLING FOR A DEGREE.

BUSINESS CENTER/HELP CENTER-

EVANGELISTS; HOMELESS RESIDENTS; LOW INCOME PUBLIC; FORIEGN MISSIONS; PASTORS CAN COME

TO ORGANIZE THEMSELVES IN A OFFICE ENVIRONMENT ON COMPUTERS;FAXES; COPIERS; 3 HOLE PUNCHERS..../THE HOMELESS AND LOW INCOME CAN

RECEIVE ASSISTANCE FILLING OUT APPLICATIONS FROM HOUSING/FOOD STAMPS/STATE/

FEDERAL ASSISTANCE. WE WILL EVEN TRY TO HAVE THE U.S.

REPS/SENATORS INQUIRE ON BEHALF OF THE APPLICANT BY FILLING OUT PRIVACY ACT RELEASE FORMS TO WORK ON THEIR BEHALF AND FOR THEIR CASE.

YOUTH CENTER-

MINORS 12-17 YEARS OF AGE WILL BE ENCOURAGED TO DO HOMEWORK; ESPECIALLY IF TUTOR HELP IS NEEDED; OUR MOTTO WILL BE "NO HOMEWORK

DONE; NO FUN". THE PARENT(S)/SHERIFF WILL SEND A LETTER OF GOOD STANDING EITHER BY HOMEWORK BEING FINISHED OR IF MINOR IS ON PROBATION; SAID

MINOR IS IN GOOD STANDING; NOT GANG RELATED/DRUG VIOLATIONS. MINORS SHALL HAVE AN ID CARD AND THE PARENT IN CHARGE WILL HAVE A PARENT

CARD. NO MINOR SHALL LEAVE THE PREMESIS WITHOUT THE CORRECT PARENT/GUARDIAN SHOWING THEIR ID WITH THE(IR) CHILD PRESENTING THEIRS.

EVANGELISM SCHOOL- ALL PREACHERS DESIRING TO PREACH IN THE CHURCH/BE A TRAVELING EVANGELIST ARE MANDATORY TO TAKE A 1 YEAR

COURSE ON HOW/WHEN/WHERE /WHAT IS EXPECTED OF AN EVANGELIST. WITHOUT THE FULL YEAR BEING ATTENDED; NO DIPLOMA WILL BE AWARDED; A PRE-

ORDAINEE MUST THEN BE A "JUDGE" AS AN INTERN FOR A YEAR; PRE-ORDAINEE AS SUCH WILL BE NAMED; WILL NOT BE A TRAVELING EVANGELIST WITHOUT A

EVANGELISM SCHOOL DIPLOMA, NO QUESTIONS ASKED, NO EXCUSES!!

ALL COURSES <u>MUST</u> BE COMPLETED; TASKS TO ATTAIN DIPLOMA WILL BE

COMPLETED OR PRE-ORDAINEE KEEPS COMING BACK THE FOLLOWING JANUARY; NO DATING AND ALL ASSIGNMENTS WILL BE COMPLETED;

CORRECTLY AND ON TIME.

<u>*F.W.MAXWELL/N.W.*</u>

<u>*MCCLISH MEMORIAL*</u>

<u>*LIBRARY-*</u> *WITH PAST HISTORY OF AMERICAN APOSTOLIC FAITH MOVEMENT SUCH*

SHALL BE A PUBLIC
LIBRARY WITH
ACCESS TO
COMPUTERS,
COPIERS, FAXES AND
PUBLIC RESTROOMS
AND QUIET STUDY
ROOMS.

MAIL CENTER- THE RULE IS "THE RESIDENT THAT RECIEVES THAT MAIL; GETS THE MAIL". THE CENTER WILL PROVIDE TO RECIEVE/SEND MAIL ON THE

ORGANIZATIONS BEHALF AND SELL POSTAGE TO THE RESIDENTS.

FUNDRAISING CENTER- SHALL RECIEVE ALL FUNDS!

FOR THE BENEFIT OF THE ORGANIZATION

BEHIND 6 INCH BULLET PROOF GLASS AND ARMED GUARDS AT THE DOOR. SUCH DONATION MONETARY/NON-MONETARY SHALL RECIEVE A RECIEPT

LAW CENTER- SHALL INHABIT UP TO 3 ATTORNEYS.

1. A CORPORATE ATTORNEY FOR THE ORGANIZATION. 2. A TAX ATTORNEY FOR THE FUND RAISING AND THE

ORGANIZATION. 3. A PERSONAL ATTORNEY FOR THE PRESIDENT. THESE WILL UPHOLD THE CONSTITUTIONAL RIGHTS OF ALL SAID PEOPLE AND BENEFIT AS SUCH INCLUDING

DEFENSE IN A COURT

OF LAW AND

UPHOLDING OF

RELIGIOUS

FREEDOMS TO

PRACTICE AND

ESTABLISH SUCH

WITHOUT THE

FOREKNOWLEDGE OF

THE FEDERAL
GOVERNMENT.
<u>POLICE/FIRE/EMT</u>
<u>OFFICES</u>- THE
ORGANIZATION'S
BUILDING TO
PROVIDE OUR LOCAL
EMERGENCY
SERVICES A PLACE TO

INHABIT FOR THE CAUSE OF THE ORGANIZATION.

<u>TRANSITIONAL HOUSING</u>- HHOPAC, INC'S APARTMENT COMPLEX FOR THOSE WHO ARE NOT READY TO GO IN THE

WORLD AS AN ADJUSTMENT FOR LIVING. 30% OF ALL INCOME WILL BE GIVEN FOR RENT. RULES WILL APPLY AGAINST DRINKING; VISITORS; DRUGS AND TOBACCO.

ORPHANAGE- IN THE EVENT A CHILD NEEDS A 24 HOUR EMERGENCY SHELTER OR A SHORT TERM STAY.

EVANGELIST DROP IN CENTER/HOUSE- IF A PASTOR HAS NO

MEANS TO GIVE

FOOD/SHOWER OR

SHARE A BATHROOM

FROM 9A TO 2 P;

ANY JESUS NAME

EVANGELIST MAY

SHOWER; HAVE

RESTROOM

PRIVILEGES;

LAUNDER CLOTHING

AND RECIEVE A MEAL

HOT OR COLD

(BROWN BAG).

"WHO WE ARE"

MAY 6,2011

WE ARE HOPE HOUSE

OF POWER

APOSTOLIC CHURCH

,INC. WE ARE A

INDEPENDENT

MINISTRY. WE ARE A

INDEPENDENT

BRANCH WORK OFF

OF LIVING WATERS

PENTECOSTAL CHURCH; PASTOR CHRISTOPHER SMITH SAVANNAH, TN 38372.

OUR CHIEF OFFICER ANSWERS ONLY TO PASTOR SMITH AT THIS TIME. THERE IS

ONLY A BOARD AT THE PLEASURE OF THE CHIEF OFFICER.

BY-LAWS CAN BE PURCHASED FOR A $5.00 LOVE OFFERING; UNLESS YOU ARE A PARISHONER WITH A

SIGNED LETTER OF AGREEMENT WITH OUR CHURCH.

(MANDATORY)

YOU MAY START ATTENDING ANY CHURCH OF YOUR CHOICE ON SUNDAY

BETWEEN 9AM AND 12 NOON OR 4P TO 10PM.(REGISTRATION FOR NEW DAY TO STAY IS AT 2PM). ANYONE AND EVERYONE THAT DOES NOT ATTEND LIVING WATERS

*PENTECOSTAL CHURCH OR HHOPAC, INC CHAPEL AT 5PM; IS PUT ON ***NOTICE***<u>YOU MUST BRING BACK A CHURCH BULLETIN SIGNED BY THE BUS DRIVER OR</u>*

PASTOR!!! (NO EXCUSES)****

SATURDAYS AT THE MISSION-

SATURDAYS AT THE MISSION IS KNOWN AS "BUNK DOWN DAY". YOUR CHORES

HAVE TO BE COMPLETED AND DONE CORRECTLY; BREAKFAST DISHES HAVE TO BE COMPLETED BY 10AM; EVERYONE HAS SHOWERED; HYGIENED AND

CLOTHES ARE WASHED;DRYED AND PUT AWAY PROPERLY;HUNG UP(POSSIBLY); ALL BEDS ARE MADE; BED AREAS ARE CLEAN; NO ONE IS IN RECLINING ROOM

TILL NOON. SNACKS AND DRINKS ARE PURCHASED THE NIGHT BEFORE W/O BEING IN BED AREA. **CHIEF OFFICER GIVES OKAY BY NOON OR BEFORE THEN OR NO BUNK DOWN DAY!!!**

"HOW WE BELIEVE"

* WE BELIEVE THAT JESUS CHRIST IS THE NAME OF GOD- MATTHEW 1:21; LUKE 2:21

*WE BELIEVE IN THE ONENESS(WE BELIEVE THAT THE TRINITY IS A DOCTRINE OF JEZEBEL)(BAAL) REVELATION 2:20-23

EPHESIANS 4:5;

DEUTERONOMY 6:4;

ISAIAH 43:11; ISAIAH 44:8; COLOSSIANS 2:9

* WE BELIEVE IN THE POWER OF THE HOLY GHOST- ACTS 2:4; ACTS 1:8; ISAIAH 6:1-4

*WE BELIEVE IN THE OPERATION OF THE GIFTS OF THE SPIRIT- 1ST CORINTHIANS 12:8-14

*WE BELIEVE ALL MANKIND HAS SINNED- GENESIS 3:1-24

*WE BELIEVE EVERYONE OF MANKIND HAS TO BE SAVED: MATTHEW 28:19; MARK 16: 15-16;LUKE 24:46-48; JOHN 3:1-6

*WE BELIEVE IN THE SIGNS TO FOLLOW THE BELIEVERS- MARK 16:17-18

*WE BELIEVE THAT ALL NEED TO SPEAK WITH TOUNGES AS A SIGN THAT YOU HAVE THE HOLY

GHOST-ACTS 2:4;
ACTS 19:1;I
CORINTHIANS 14:18;
1ST CORINTHAINS
14:40

*WE BELIEVE EVERY
MAN NEEDS TO OR
CAN BE HEALED-
JAMES 5:14-

15(PHYSICAL;SPIRITU
AL;FINANCIAL;MENT
AL;EMOTIONAL)

*WE BELIEVE THAT
THE 10
COMMANDMENTS
ARE THE LAWS
WRITTEN IN STONE;
BESIDES THE SPOKEN

BY CHRIST ON EARTH AND WRITTEN; EXODOUS 20:1-14; MATTHEW CH'S. 5-7

*WE BELIEVE THAT PRAYER IS A IMPORTANT PART OF OUR RELATIONSHIP

WITH GOD-
MATTHEW 6:6-9

*WE BELIEVE JESUS
IS OUR SUPREME
EXAMPLE- MATTHEW
3:14-17

*WE BELIEVE JESUS
SENT US OUT TO DO
HIS WORK AND

THERE ARE RULES THAT WE MUST ABIDE BY IN MORALE/KEEP FROM SIN; MATTHEW 10: 5-14; 1ST TIMOTHY 3:1-15

*WE BELIEVE WE MUST INVOKE OUR

CIVIC DUTIES(PAYING OF LOCAL/COUNTY/STATE/FEDERAL TAXES;JURY DUTY; CITIZEN ARREST; TESTIFY IN COURT; ETC.)-MATTHEW 22:17-21

*WE BELIEVE BOTH MEN AND WOMEN CAN BE PART OF THE MINISTRY- GALATIANS 3:28; LUKE 2:37-39

*WE BELIEVE THAT EVERY PERSON SHOULD LIVE

ACCORDING TO THE LIGHT THEY SEE(STANDARDS; HOLY LIVING)- ROMANS 12:3

*WE BELIEVE WE ARE IN SPIRITUAL WARFARE- (EPHESIANS 6:10-18)

*WE BELIEVE TO GIVE 10% OF OUR INCREASE(TITHES); WE BELIEVE TO PAY OUR OFFERING; EVEN SEED OFFERING; WE BELIEVE TO PAY THE (HALF-SHEKEL) 5%

ADDED TO THE 10% IN THE EVENT WE DON'T PAY TITHES (TO REDEEM OUR OFFERING)(EVEN OUR SOULS FROM THE CURSE.) WE BELIEVE THE TITHES GOES TO THE HANDS

OF THE PASTOR; NOT THE OFFERING PLATE NOR SECRETARY.

MALACHI 3:10; LEVITICUS 23:9-11;MATTHEW 22:21; NUMBERS 27:15;31; LEVITICUS 10:15;

LUKE 21:1-4;MARK 4:3,8

OUR OPERATIONS- FROM 2PM-9AM:

WE OFFER SCRIPTURAL ADVISEMENT; CHAPEL SERVICES; A DINNER AND

BREAKFAST MEAL; HYGENIC TIMES; LAUNDERING; A BED TO SLEEP.

WE CLOSE AT 9AM DAILY; WE ARE CLOSED THURSDAY AND SUNDAY UNTIL THE FOLLOWING

BUSNIESS DAY AT 2PM.

WE ARE CLOSED ON AUGUST 31ST OF EVERY YEAR.

WE ARE CLOSED FOR THANKSGIVING AND CHRISTMAS FOR A WEEK OR TWO

WEEKS OF EVERY YEAR. (EXAMPLE: THE FRIDAY BEFORE THE WEEK OF CHRISTMAS TILL JANUARY 4TH OF THE FOLLOWING NEW YEAR)

WE OFFER RIDES TO LIVING WATERS PENTECOSTAL CHURCH @ 7PM ON THURSDAY AND 2PM ON SUNDAY.

THE FOLLOWING ARE RECOGNIZED FOR STAFF/OFFICERS NOT

NECESSARILY EMPLOYED OR PAID-

REV.STEPHEN C. MAXWELL-PREZ/CHIEF OFFICER

PASTOR CHRIS SMITH-MOTHER CHURCH PASTOR

LIVING WATERS PENTECOSTAL CHURCH

REV. JEAN SIMMONS-SECRETARY OF MOTHER CHURCH

LIVING WATERS PENTECOSTAL CHURCH

REV. JANE SMITH-TREASURER OF MOTHER CHURCH

LIVING WATERS PENTECOSTAL CHURCH.

CORPORATE INFO- (INC.)

MAY 6TH 2011- CREATED/BEGAN

CHARTERED IN TN- #657690

EIN/TIN:#35-2398423

(MONETARY CONTRIBUTIONS FOR GIFT)

THANK YOU FOR YOUR PURCHASES OF THE FOLLOWING EITHER FROM MYSELF OR

WWW.CREATESPACE
.COM-

www.createspace.co
m/3998123

"BY-LAWS OF
HHOPAC,INC"

www.createspace.co
m/3994374

"TRIBULATION, WHAT IT MIGHT BE"

www.createspace.com/3979631

"THE BOOK OF STEPHEN;PROPHETIC WORDS OF THE LORD JESUS; VOL 1

www.createspace.co
m/3988061

"THE HANDBOOK OF
EVANGELISTS"

www.createspace.co
m/3979661

"MORTON AND
MORE MORTON"

www.creatspace.com/3986003

"THE FUNNIEST STORIES I HAVE EVER HEARD/FAMILY STORIES"

www.createspace.com/3980085

"HEARTBREAK IN THE THRONE ROOM"

www.createspace.com/3988159

"HAMBURGERS;FRIES AND YOU"

www.createspace.com/3998366

"THE BOOK OF STEPHEN; PROPHETIC WORDS OF THE LORD JESUS ; VOL 2

www.createspace.com/3999071

"NONSENSE...WHAT DO YOU THINK YOUR DOING OR TALKING

ABOUT;

PENTECOSTALS

EXPLAINED"

www.createspace.co

m/4001165

"SUNDAY SCHOOL

LESSONS MADE

EASY"

www.createspace.com/4003071

"THE LAWS OF TITHES AND OFFERINGS"

www.createspace.com/4003073

"YOUR PERFECT RIGHT TO KNOW"

BOOKS PURCHASED FROM MYSELF ARE 1/$5.00;2/$9.00; 3/$12.00 AND EACH ADDITIONAL BOOK IS $5.00 EACH. THANKS!

POST OFFICE BOX 331

SAVANNAH, TN

38372

stephenmaxwellmini

stries@yahoo.com

NOTE(YOUR PERSONAL CHECK MUST HAVE YOUR DL/STATE ID # AND PHONE # THANK YOU)

www.ingramcontent.com/pod-product-compliance
Lightning Source LLC
Chambersburg PA
CBHW022102170526
45157CB00004B/1449